Mr. & Mrs. Hay the Horse

By Allan Ahlberg
Illustrated by Colin McNaughton

GOLDEN PRESS • NEW YORK
Western Publishing Company, Inc.
Racine, Wisconsin

First published in the United Kingdom by Puffin Books/Kestrel Books.
Published in the U.S.A. in 1982.

Library of Congress Catalog Card Number: 81-84173
ISBN 0-307-31704-8 / ISBN 0-307-61704-1 (lib. bdg.)
A B C D E F G H I J

Mr. and Mrs. Hay were a horse.
Mr. Hay was the front end.
Mrs. Hay was the back end.
They worked in a circus,
and on the stage.

Now Mr. and Mrs. Hay
had not always been a horse.
When they first met,
Mr. Hay was a tree
and Mrs. Hay was a chicken.

But soon they fell in love,
got married—and bought a horse suit.

As the years went by,
Mr. and Mrs. Hay had two children.
There was a boy named Henry.
There was a girl named Henrietta.
When the children were little,
they were very happy.

They rode on their mom and dad's back.
They laughed at their mom and dad's tricks.
They were as proud as could be.
   "Our mom and dad are a horse!"
they told everybody.

But later on,
when the children were older,
the trouble began.

Henry and Henrietta were embarrassed
by their mom and dad.
The trouble was, Mr. and Mrs. Hay
liked being a horse.
They went everywhere in their horse suit.
They liked galloping about.

Other moms and dads
were more sensible.
The moms wore dresses
and baked apple pies.
The dads dug the gardens
and took the dogs for a walk.

Mr. and Mrs. Hay did not
take their dog for a walk.
They took him for a ride!

So Henry and Henrietta
tried to get their parents
to be like other parents.
  "Would you like a job
in an office, Dad?" asked Henrietta.

"Would you like to work
in a shop, Mom?" Henry asked.
They even hid the horse suit.
But it was no use.
Mr. and Mrs. Hay soon found the suit.
And things did not get better.
They got worse.

There was trouble at school, too.
When other moms and dads
came to see the teacher,
they waited quietly.

When Mr. and Mrs. Hay
came to see the teacher,
they galloped about.

Now once a year the school
had a Christmas Show.
A magician came to do
his tricks for the children.

The moms and dads were also invited.
   Henry and Henrietta were pleased
about the show.
But they were worried, too.
   "The other moms and dads
will come in their best clothes
and be sensible," they said.
"Our mom and dad will be galloping
around in a horse suit!"

On the night of the show
Henry and Henrietta went
to school early.

They helped to get the stage ready.
They put the chairs out.

By half-past seven most of the people
were in their seats.

But Mr. and Mrs. Hay were late.
Henry and Henrietta
could not see them anywhere.

Then the head of the school stepped
onto the stage.
He was looking worried.

"Ladies and gentlemen,
boys and girls!" he said.
"I am sorry to say
there will be no show tonight!
The magician cannot come.
He had to take his rabbits to the vet."

All the moms and dads looked sad.
The children looked sad, too.
A baby in the front row began to cry.
Then, suddenly, there was
the sound of a galloping horse.
Onto the stage came Mr. and Mrs. Hay!

"Oh, dear," said Henry and Henrietta.
They felt their cheeks
getting hot and red.
But soon Mr. and Mrs. Hay
were doing their tricks.
They began to sing songs, too.

They even danced—and told jokes!
The baby in the front row
began to laugh.
All the children laughed.
And the parents cheered
and clapped their hands.

Henry and Henrietta
began to feel better.
When the head of the school said,
"Three cheers for Mr. and Mrs. Hay!"
they felt better still.

The other children all said,
"We wish *our* moms and dads
were horses!"

Henry and Henrietta were as proud
as could be!

Two nights later,
when Henry and Henrietta
were fast asleep,
a funny Santa Claus
crept into their room.
This Santa Claus had
lots of presents for the children.
But there was one special present.
It was just what Henry and Henrietta
wanted most of all . . .

. . . a little horse suit!

The End